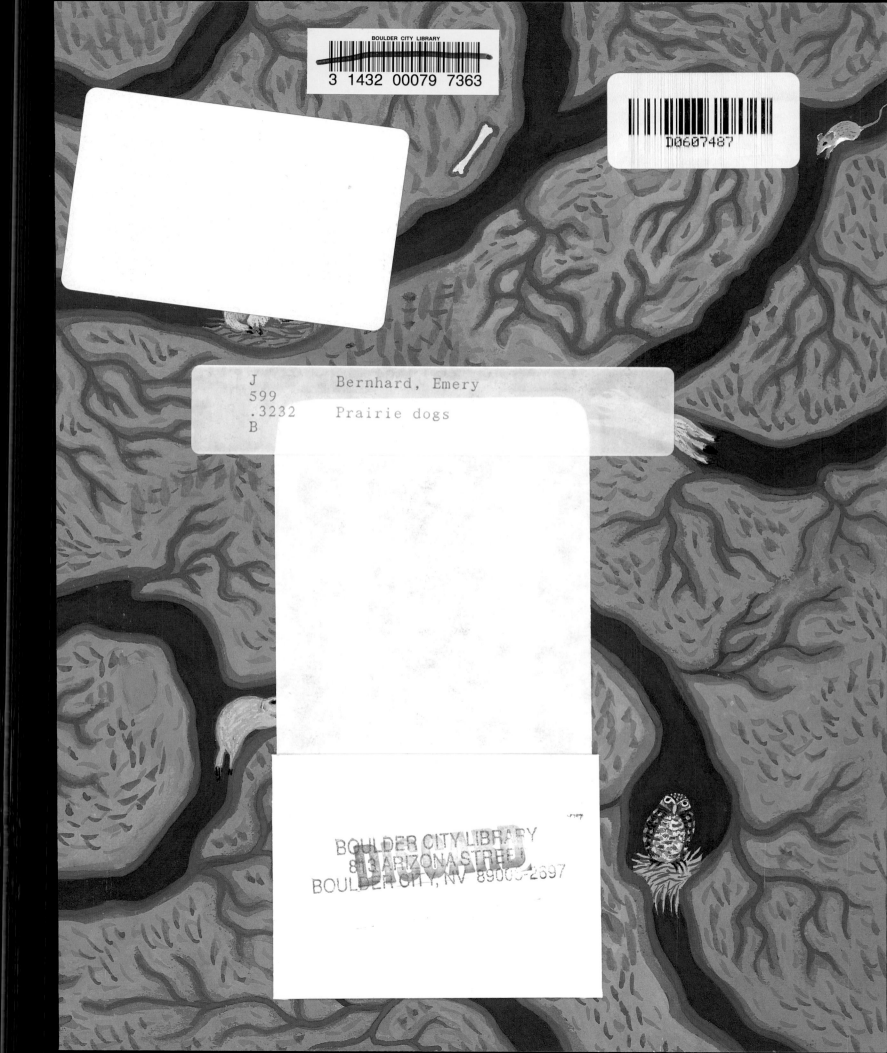

Prairie Dogs

Written by EMERY BERNHARD
Illustrated by DURGA BERNHARD

Gulliver Books
Harcourt Brace & Company
San Diego   New York   London

Gulliver Books is a registered trademark of Harcourt Brace & Company.

Library of Congress Cataloging-in-Publication Data
Bernhard, Emery.
Prairie dogs/written by Emery Bernhard; illustrated by Durga Bernhard.
p. cm.
"Gulliver Books."
Summary: Describes the physical characteristics, social behavior, and
reputation as a pest of this grassland rodent.
ISBN 0-15-201286-9
1. Prairie dogs—Juvenile literature. [1. Prairie dogs.] I. Bernhard, Durga, ill.
II. Title.
QL737.R68B47   1997
599.32'32—dc20   96-22849

First edition
A C E F D B

Printed in Singapore

The illustrations in this book were done in Winsor & Newton gouache
on Whatman 140-pound cold-press watercolor paper.
The display type was set in Colwell.
The text type was set in Stone Serif.
Color separations by Bright Arts, Ltd., Singapore
Printed and bound by Tien Wah Press, Singapore
This book was printed on totally chlorine-free Nymolla Matte Art paper.
Production supervision by Stanley Redfern and Ginger Boyer
Designed by Lydia D'moch

For Margit

It is just after sunrise on the plains east of the Rocky Mountains. Loud, high-pitched barks repeat across the grassland. The prairie dogs have seen an intruder. All around, black-tailed prairie dogs peek out from their burrow entrances. Their golden tan color blends with the earth as they look over their territory.

Prairie dogs are rodents, not dogs. They belong to the squirrel family, which includes chipmunks, marmots, and woodchucks.

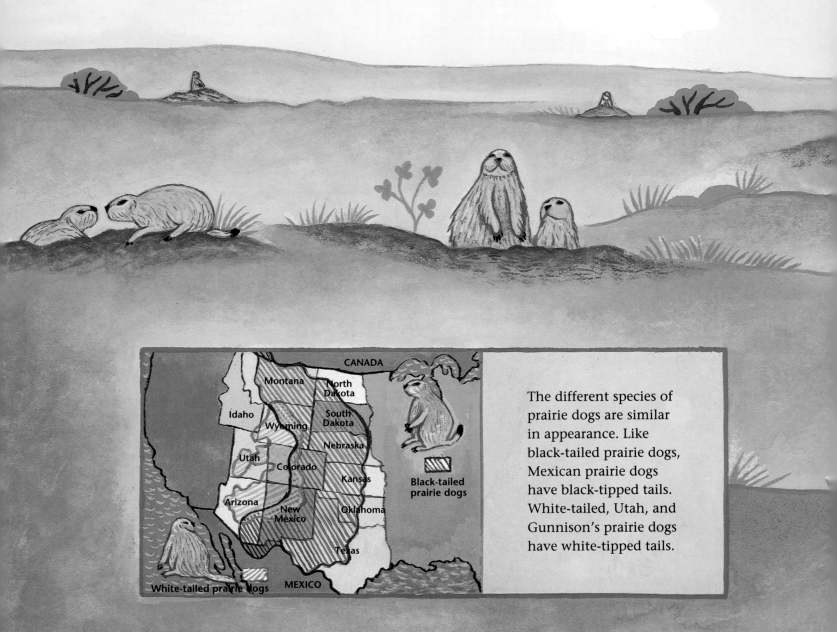

The different species of prairie dogs are similar in appearance. Like black-tailed prairie dogs, Mexican prairie dogs have black-tipped tails. White-tailed, Utah, and Gunnison's prairie dogs have white-tipped tails.

Of the five kinds of prairie dogs, the black-tailed is by far the most common. Black-tails live in the prairies of the central and western Great Plains of North America, which stretch from southern Canada to northern Mexico. Plump, with furry bodies and stubby tails, they grow to lengths of eleven to sixteen inches and weigh from one to three pounds, about twice as much as their sleek cousins, the tree squirrels.

Animals such as the tiger salamander often make their homes in prairie dog burrows.

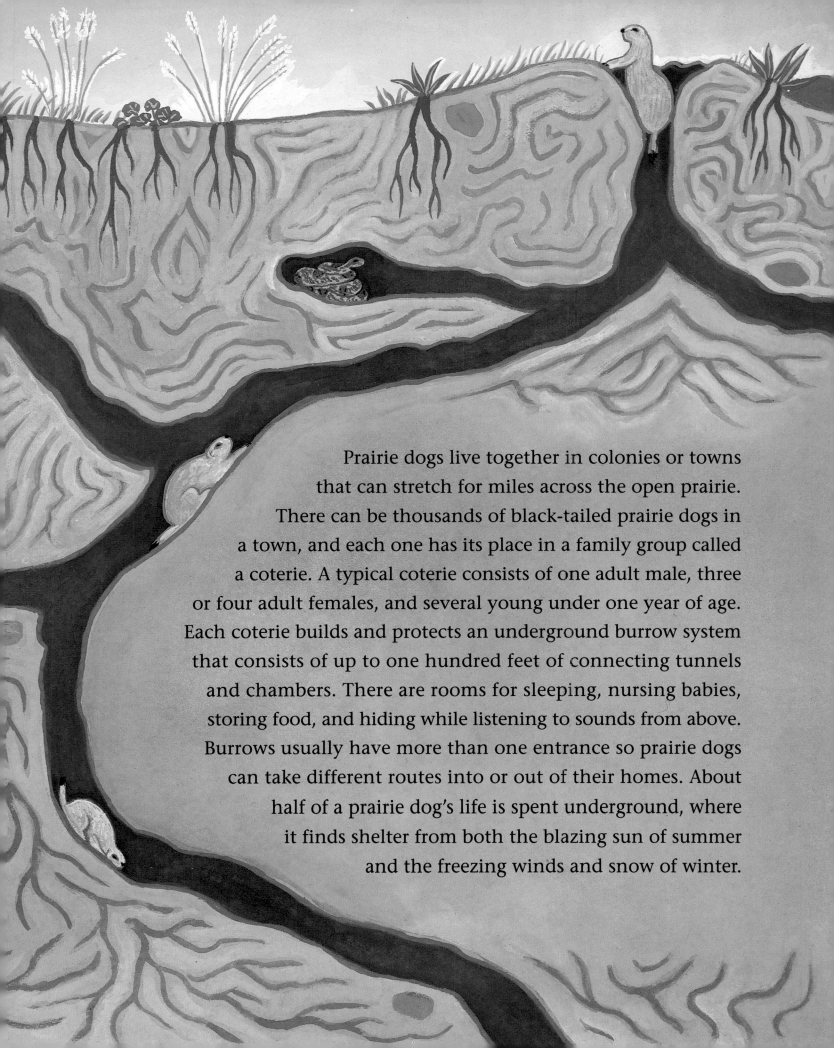

Prairie dogs live together in colonies or towns
that can stretch for miles across the open prairie.
There can be thousands of black-tailed prairie dogs in
a town, and each one has its place in a family group called
a coterie. A typical coterie consists of one adult male, three
or four adult females, and several young under one year of age.
Each coterie builds and protects an underground burrow system
that consists of up to one hundred feet of connecting tunnels
and chambers. There are rooms for sleeping, nursing babies,
storing food, and hiding while listening to sounds from above.
Burrows usually have more than one entrance so prairie dogs
can take different routes into or out of their homes. About
half of a prairie dog's life is spent underground, where
it finds shelter from both the blazing sun of summer
and the freezing winds and snow of winter.

To build their burrows, prairie dogs use their sharp teeth to cut through roots and their long front claws and short, strong legs to dig, scrape, push, and pile soil. Using earth dug out while tunneling, they build mounds around their burrow entrances. The mounds provide elevated lookouts, where the prairie dogs can scan for predators, and prevent water from entering the tunnels during heavy rains.

Prairie dogs are especially busy after it rains. They shape and pound the wet soil around their burrows into place with the points of their noses, leaving nose prints in the mounds.

Prairie dogs have keen eyesight and hearing. From dawn to dusk, as they forage for food and maintain their burrows, they are on the lookout for predators such as hawks, eagles, bobcats, coyotes, weasels, foxes, and humans. While in their burrows, prairie dogs are safe from most predators, but at night they can do little to defend themselves against ferrets, who can easily slip into the prairie dog tunnels, and badgers, who can dig out their underground prey.

An alert prairie dog spots an approaching hawk when it is still only a dot in the sky. The prairie dog barks a loud warning, which signals everyone to locate the predator and—if necessary—to dive into their burrows.

Sometimes prairie dogs fight back against small predators. A hawk perched on a mound in a prairie dog town may be rammed, an attacking weasel may be chased away by a mob of angry black-tails, and a snake invading a burrow may be bitten or buried in flying dirt.

Once their enemy has left, prairie dogs around the town begin to leap upright. They throw their front feet high and give a wheezing, whistling yip that seems to say, "This is *my* territory, and all is clear!" Scientists call this the jump-yip display.

When prairie dogs meet, they sometimes greet each other with open mouths and touch each other's teeth in a way that resembles kissing. If they are members of the same coterie, they often begin to stroke each other. They clean one another's fur by scratching through it with their claws and by nibbling with their teeth. Grooming helps prairie dogs get to know the scent and touch of members of the coterie. It also gets rid of fleas, lice, and ticks.

The greeting given to a visitor from a different coterie is not as friendly. If prairie dogs smell a stranger, they may flare their tails, chatter their teeth, charge, and even bite.

Sometimes a male prairie dog will invade a neighboring coterie and challenge the dominant male. If the dominant male is weak or does not defend his territory, the invading male may take over the coterie.

Young prairie dogs follow adults around, crawling under their bodies and begging to be groomed.

Black-tailed prairie dogs breed as the winter nears its end, in February and March. It is time to be busy again after months spent mostly resting and eating the food stored in their burrows. Soft, low barks are heard around the prairie dog town as the males try to attract females who are ready to breed.

After mating, both males and females clean out the old burrows and dig new tunnels. Then the pregnant females line their nesting chambers with soft, dry grass to make nursery nests for the babies that will soon be born.

Pregnant females may spend an hour at a time collecting mouthfuls of grass for their nurseries. Prairie dog pregnancies are thirty-four or thirty-five days long.

Newborn pups

Born in litters of four or five pups, prairie dog babies enter the world wrinkled, hairless, blind, and weighing only about half an ounce. But the pups grow quickly nursing on their mother's milk. In three weeks their fur has grown in. At five weeks they open their eyes. By the sixth week they have begun to run and bark. It is time to leave the burrow.

Pups at three weeks

By seven weeks the pups weigh about four ounces and have begun to eat plants. By watching adults, they learn which plants to eat and where to hide if they hear a warning bark. The pups are free to leave the territory of the home coterie and explore the whole town. Running from one burrow to another, they romp, wrestle, tumble, and chase each other. The youngsters are tolerated unless they interfere with an adult who is trying to eat or keep watch. Pups that are a nuisance are given a sharp nip or a shove!

Pups at six weeks

Nursing mothers lick and stroke their babies. They remain with their pups almost constantly and allow no one else to come near, until the pups are ready to leave the burrow.

When pups practice the jump-yip display, they often leap up too fast, throw their front feet too high, lean back too far—and end up toppling over backward!

A prairie dog nips a scarlet globe mallow close
to the ground and then sits up, holding the flower
in its front paws and nibbling away. Prairie dogs
also eat seeds and, sometimes, grasshoppers.

Plants on the prairie grow rapidly in the summer, but the grasses in a prairie dog town are never long. This is because prairie dogs eat the grasses and other leafy plants that grow around their burrow mounds, keeping the vegetation well trimmed and giving themselves a good view of their territory.

Over time the constant pruning of prairie grasses encourages the growth of a variety of young plants. Tender new grass is more nutritious and digestible than the rougher, taller, older grass found elsewhere on the prairie. Grazing animals such as bison and antelope are attracted to the succulent shoots that thrive in prairie dog towns.

While grazing in prairie dog towns, the shaggy bison also find relief from heat and biting insects. To cool off and shed bugs, the bison paw at the dirt around burrows and loosen it with their horns. Then they lie down and roll in the loose dirt. This dust bathing, or wallowing, may at first smash the prairie dogs' entrance mounds, but the shallow holes it leaves behind collect rainwater and foster the growth of broad-leaved plants. Because prairie dogs eat these plants, both the bison and the prairie dogs benefit from their relationship.

More than 170 different animals are active around the natural communities found in prairie dog towns. Many of them rely on prairie dogs for either food or shelter.

The prairie dogs' dark burrows provide cozy homes for ants, beetles, fleas, crickets, mice, rabbits, and salamanders. Spiders—including the black widow—often build webs over burrow entrances. Burrowing owls make their nests in vacant burrows and may have to share them with prairie voles, thirteen-lined ground squirrels, or black-footed ferrets. Black-footed ferrets, which are very rare, also depend on prairie dogs as prey.

Badger

Black-footed ferret

Short-horned grasshopper

Thirteen-lined ground squirrel

Prairie rattlesnake

By the end of their first summer of foraging, prairie dog pups are almost full grown. Through playing and grooming, they have become familiar with the members of their coterie. They are no longer welcome in other territories. Fall will soon arrive. Now the major activity of young prairie dogs is eating to store fat for winter.

In the spring some black-tails will move on in search of food, space, or mates. After spending their first winter at home, one-

year-old female prairie dogs may leave to join other coteries. Many yearling males will also leave their old burrows and relocate to abandoned burrows, or dig new ones at the edge of the town, where they may breed and establish coteries of their own.

The female prairie dogs will live for up to seven years, while the males—who are mainly responsible for the defense of their coteries' territories—usually do not survive for more than five years.

Because they do not hibernate, black-tailed prairie dogs were once a valuable addition to the winter diet of the Plains Indians. Even when the herds of bison and antelope were scattered by winter storms, prairie dogs could still be found.

According to the mythology of the Cheyenne and the Lakota Indians, people did not always hunt animals for food. In fact, when the world was new, four-legged creatures hunted two-legged creatures, including human beings. Then a great race was held between the four-leggeds and the two-leggeds to determine who would have the privilege of hunting. We all know who won.

Of course, each of the four-leggeds had its own reason for losing. And can you guess why Prairie Dog lost? Because instead of running, he wasted his time barking, snarling, and yipping at the other animals in the race—especially Hawk.

Over the course of the 1800s, the prairie saw great change. The Plains Indians were driven from their homes as settlers intent on farming, mining, and cattle ranching spread across the land. By the turn of the century, the Lakota were confined to reservations. The grasslands were being converted to croplands and pastures, and the huge herds of bison were gone, replaced with herds of cattle. But there were still millions of prairie dogs.

Many of the settlers became convinced that prairie dogs were competing with cows for grass and endangering horses and cows,

which might step into prairie dog burrows and break their legs. Ranchers and government agencies teamed up to rid grazing land of prairie dogs. By the early 1970s, remaining black-tailed towns were widely separated and hemmed in. Black-footed ferrets, who live only in prairie dog towns, were in danger of extinction. It was then that scientists and some ranchers began to question whether prairie dogs are pests. Now prairie dogs are protected in wildlife refuges and national parks, but their numbers have been severely reduced.

Prairie dogs, black-footed ferrets, and other unique animals and plants will not survive without the preservation of large areas of their prairie habitat.

What might happen if prairie dogs were not considered pests? Many ranchers insist that there is scarcely enough grass for their cattle and that they cannot afford to allow prairie dogs on their land. Conservationists argue that overgrazing is caused not by prairie dogs but by cows left to graze in the same fenced areas for long periods. They point out that in the long run, prairie dogs enrich the soil by leaving droppings and by bringing dried grasses and weeds underground for their nests.

Is there enough food on the range for cows *and* prairie dogs? Some ranchers—in cooperation with government wildlife biologists—have begun to tolerate a limited number of prairie dogs on their land. But most ranchers have yet to be convinced, and it is too soon to tell whether ranchers, cattle, and prairie dogs can share the prairie.

Scientists have found that cattle put on about the same weight whether they are grazed in prairie dog towns or on grasslands where prairie dogs have—at great expense—been exterminated.

GLOSSARY

breed: To mate and produce offspring.

burrow: A hole or tunnel dug by an animal for shelter.

coterie (KOH-ti-ree): A small family group of prairie dogs.

dominant male: A powerful male animal that is the leader of a group.

exterminate: To destroy or get rid of all the members of a group or type of animal.

extinction: The complete elimination of a type of plant or animal from the earth.

fertilize: To add to the soil nutrients that help plants grow.

forage: To search for food.

habitat: The environment or place where a particular plant or animal lives.

pest: A troublesome animal that destroys plants or animals that people use.

predator: An animal that hunts and kills other animals for food.

prey: An animal that is hunted and killed by another for food.

territory: An area that is claimed and defended by an animal or group of animals, and that may be used for shelter, breeding, and feeding.

yearling: An animal between one and two years old.

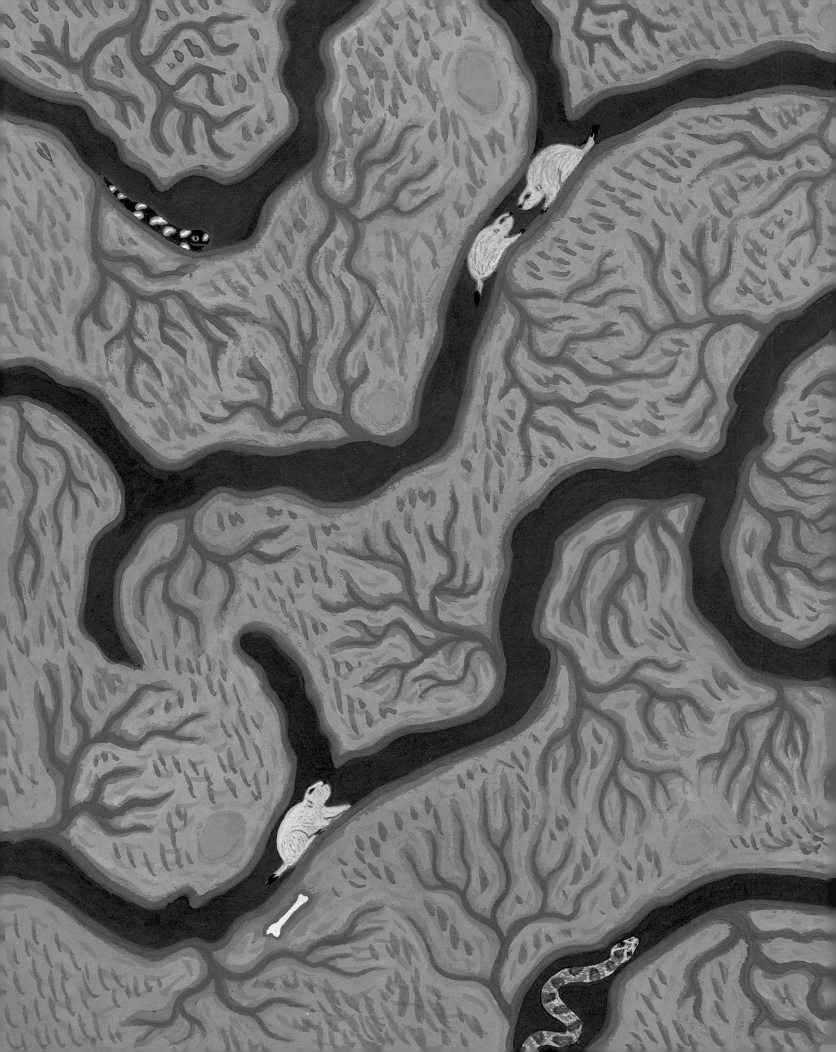